Hospital

An Art Project by Robert Priseman

Paintings by Robert Priseman
With essays by Professor Margaret Iversen
and Dr Ben Cranfield

An Essay by
Professor Margaret Iversen

Robert Priseman
The Aesthetics of De-Personalization

Robert Priseman's paintings present us with 'a strange new beauty'. This resonant phrase is Mallarmé's -- a poet who favored a depersonalized way of writing that valued the intrinsically poetic domain of language. Mallarmé wrote an appreciative account of Manet, praising the way his hand became "an impersonal abstraction... The artist's personal feeling, his particular tastes are, for the time being, absorbed, ignored." Manet is determined to paint "entirely without himself." Searching for a way to accomplish this feat, Manet looked to the Dutch and Flemish artists, famous for their patient, self-less observation of the world, and to an artist who had absorbed their lessons -- Velasquez. This aesthetic of de-personalization is fundamentally about displacing one's own agency, cutting through habitual stereotypes and sentiment, so that something other can surface.

There is a long tradition of art-making that aims at depersonalization. Although it is not possible to achieve, what is desired is the elocutionary disappearance of the artist. As a result, his work lacks all trace of emotional involvement and expressive gesture. Of course, that does not mean that the work is devoid of emotion. On the contrary, it may mean that quite violent emotion is only just held in check.

Roland Barthes gave the name 'writing degree zero' to a kind of prose first identified by Sartre in a review of Camus's *The Stranger*, where he described the prose as neutral or colorless --écriture blanche. Barthes, alluding mainly to Robbe-Grillet, compared this style of prose to a journalist's writing, but only in so far as the journalist refrains form emotive language. The idea, he suggests, 'was to go beyond Literature by entrusting one's fate to a sort of basic speech', without style. Many contemporary artists also aspire to a neutral, flat quasi-journalistic style – a sort of zero degree of image making. The work of the German painter Gerhard Richter is a good example.

Robert Priseman's paintings have something in common with Richter's. First, and most obviously, there is the evident use of photography as an intermediary, distancing device. It would seem that for many artists, painting is only possible today given the mediation of photography. Photography's "objective" vision of the world has often been celebrated; mechanization is understood not only as a way of cutting through the carapace of our habitual, interest-laden perceptions, but also as a way of circumventing the weight of artistic convention. Richter's remarks suggest that, for him, the photograph is capable of a more objective, direct or neutral vision than painting from a model. He was drawn to ordinary snap shots without pretension and 'devoid of style.' – the basic speech of visual representation. For him, photography avoids the distortion of style and the weight of artistic convention. The all-over blurring of the painted image is also a means of neutralization. This blurring has a counterpart in Priseman's systematic elimination of detail. In this, there is also a link with Edward Hopper whose paintings derive their intensity and curious sense of alienation from the elimination of all distracting, inessential material. A more recent prominent artist who comes to mind in this connection is Thomas Demand who photographs elaborately constructed paper models of interiors which often have a ghastly aura of some past atrocity about them.

The highly technical, craftsmanly nature of Priseman's painting is another way of mediating or distancing the image. The photographic source is elaborated by drawing painstaking perspectival projections. He has commented on his admiration for Vermeer's painting and the way his use of perspective seems to contain or control his sensitivity to the world. Vermeer's light is another source of inspiration for Priseman who is clearly fascinated by the play of light, both natural and, increasingly, artificial. Recently he has even been painting sources of light, like the large lighting fixture in a Jubilee Line Station.

Richter's search for visual indifference is at odds with the nature of many of his subjects: family snapshots, death and recent German history. And this is another point of contact with Priseman. The subjects of the paintings are haunted by violence and death. The hospital interiors convey a sense of foreboding precisely because they are drained of life. The visible world is pinned like a dead butterfly to the surface of the canvas where one can inspect it. It is striking that this non-expressionist artist should be attracted to the work of Francis Bacon, apparently at the very opposite end of the artistic spectrum to Priseman. However, as is well known, Bacon worked from photographic material as well. Priseman pays homage to Bacon in pristine interiors of his former house in Wivenhoe, Essex, *68 Queens Road*, but also in his *The Death of George Dyer* – a depiction of the bathroom in which Bacon's petty criminal, violent lover met his death from an overdose. Bacon's painting of the same incident, *Triptych May-June 1973*, shows a figure in a simplified architectural space, seen at three moments, culminating in a figure slumped, dead, on the toilet. Priseman's version of the event is devoid of figures, but the toilet itself seems to crouch in the corner of an otherwise empty space. The title and the emptiness prompt the imagination to supply the narrative. As Barthes said, the death of the author, brings about the birth of the reader or, in this case, the spectator.

Margaret Iversen, 2008

Mallarmé, "The Impressionists and Edouard Manet," 17. See my note 8. Daily Practice, p.31.

An Essay by
Dr Ben Cranfield

Looking Back without Anger: Robert Priseman's places of gentle trauma

A piece, such as Robert Priseman's *Threshold*, takes on a maternal role, holding the viewer in the presence of terror, whilst offering comfort with an order constructed on the edge of total life changing chaos and destruction.

Holding one's breath in front of the image, allowing the emptiness to persist, it is possible to enter Priseman's work without falling into the trap of prejudice against his subjects – bland spaces of little evocation and, contrarily, spaces of unnerving indifference. Pausing before entering the morgue, the operating theatre or utilitarian corridor, the viewer is able to get a glimpse of a different position, suggested by the careful rendering of delicate brush strokes, the angelic halo of an electric light, the openness and humility of perspective, which allows us to wander with ease around the achingly empty and lonely spaces depicted. The success of Priseman's painting lies within the contradictions of opposites – fragility with assurance, detail with minimalism, life with death, overflowing meaning with emptiness. There is an absence, however, of the melodrama and tragedy of Edward Hopper or Paul Winstanley and certainly Richter's imprisoned sense of the past is absent. But there is a relationship there with all three artists, especially in the use of the photograph to cool the emotional heat, to detach to a state of sublime concentration. There is also a great sense of stage-management, which has the feeling of gravity present in the detail of a Jeff Wall composition. The objects have been moved, the colours gently altered, writing erased, so one scene becomes a more universal metaphor, as in *The Death of George Dyer*; this is the place where George Dyer died, but it is also the most ordinary bathroom you can imagine. It is the care lavished on the scene, the almost caressing brush marks, which tell us that we must attach to this place a greater importance; an historic significance of almost epic proportions.

Priseman felt compelled to make a shift in his work as an artist – surprisingly moving from his previous profession as portrait painter to the exploration of 'empty' spaces. Such a marked shift, forces us to take notice. Even if we are unaware of this biographical detail the specific and intense contemplation of unlikely spaces also demands attention. We cannot help but ask why? This is underscored by the poised care in which the works are constructed and by their imposing scale. It is this poise and consideration, almost admiration, which marks them out, say, against the large, but gut-wrenchingly bland images of Luc Tuyman – whose relationship with the photograph is one of post-apocalyptic ambivalence, absurdity and confusion. Priseman is coming at his subjects from an almost diametrically opposed position. Whereas the shady, starched and painful environments of the Nazi regime and the holocaust act as potential contextual background for Tuyman's work, Priseman's relationship with the hospital and the generic non-space is one of awe, safety, fragility, magnitude and comfort – all at once. These works chart a style and architecture of an almost forgotten ideology; that of the post-war welfare state. At one time all would have been able to read such starkly lit and uniform spaces as the sign of progress, whereas we, as the jaded inheritors of a broken dream, have now become uncomfortable with a societal simplicity represented by such an aesthetic.

The tension between knowing and not knowing is played out in the work as a battle between minimalism and illustration. The influence of Dan Flavin is clear in Priseman's homage to tube lighting, but it is also present in the simplification of the colour field and the accentuation of that which is naturally minimal. A hospital door becomes an archetype of plastic monolithic form. A patterned floor becomes a field for infinite expansion. However, Priseman, also has a gift for narrative and at times breathes a narrative life into an empty space. There is a stylistic shifting in the work dependent on the subject matter, which plays out this fine balance between intentions. The minimal style comes into play within the institutionalised settings of Priseman's hospitals, corridors, waiting rooms, and transient spaces, with the more illustrative style emerging within the personal and particular spaces of studios, bathrooms, and hallways. This suggests the strange contradiction in the work; there is a beauty within the secure and organised spaces of an institution, but that minimal perfection comes at a cost, and no personal life or story can pervade its sterile and polished walls. In contradistinction, the porous spaces of dated hotel rooms, and long deserted studios still seem to hold the echoes of personal tragedy. This dichotomy that exists within the different positionings of Priseman's objects of study suggests his particular relationship to painting. He allows a non-premeditated stylistic device to emerge from within the therapeutic and confessional relationship of artist and image, hence the subtle shifting between the illustrative and the minimal from canvas to canvas.

The choice of hospitals as subject matter is not so surprising, as Priseman has had personal experience of places of medical care. Regardless of this the ambiguity of these environments, which can give life and mediate death, are of obvious pertinence to Priseman's use of painting as a site of ambivalent, quiet and sustained enquiry. His most recent series, however, is at first a more perplexing choice. In his series of pieces relating to the life of Francis Bacon, Priseman seems to show that homage can take many forms, as can painterly truth. Concerned with detailing spaces which have no intrinsic meaning unless accompanied by knowledge of Bacon's life and loves, Priseman diligently obtained permission to photograph Parisian hotel rooms and Spanish hospitals. The result is a strange and elusive series of work which avoids narrative simplification, but is replete with pregnant pauses and lingering, meaningful glances. The illustrative style employed here works in reverse to the minimal style used elsewhere. The lack of narrative detail within the scenes, as Priseman found them, left him with the task of making personal that which was profoundly cleansed of any significance. One of the most intriguing pieces in this series is Bacon's studio as recreated behind the glass of a museum exhibit at the Hugh Lane Gallery, Dublin. Rather than entering this false space as a real one and making the most of the fullness of information there, Priseman chooses to cast a view of the studio at a distance, the generic corridor with high shine floor taking up the majority of the canvas. The result is an image at once laden with suggestive significance, with the goal of full autobiographical knowledge tantalisingly out of reach. The historical is left undone, we are imprisoned on this side of the temporal glass, with this most enigmatic, and charismatic of twentieth century figures lost on his side. Both sides of Priseman's paintings, therefore, seem to draw the same conclusion; that the painting of an image is like the tracing of ones fingers over a cold stone death mask in the darkness of church – it leaves one with a sense of presentness and profound loss at the same time.

Ben Cranfield, 2008

The Paintings

Corridor 153cm x 153cm, Oil on linen, date 2004

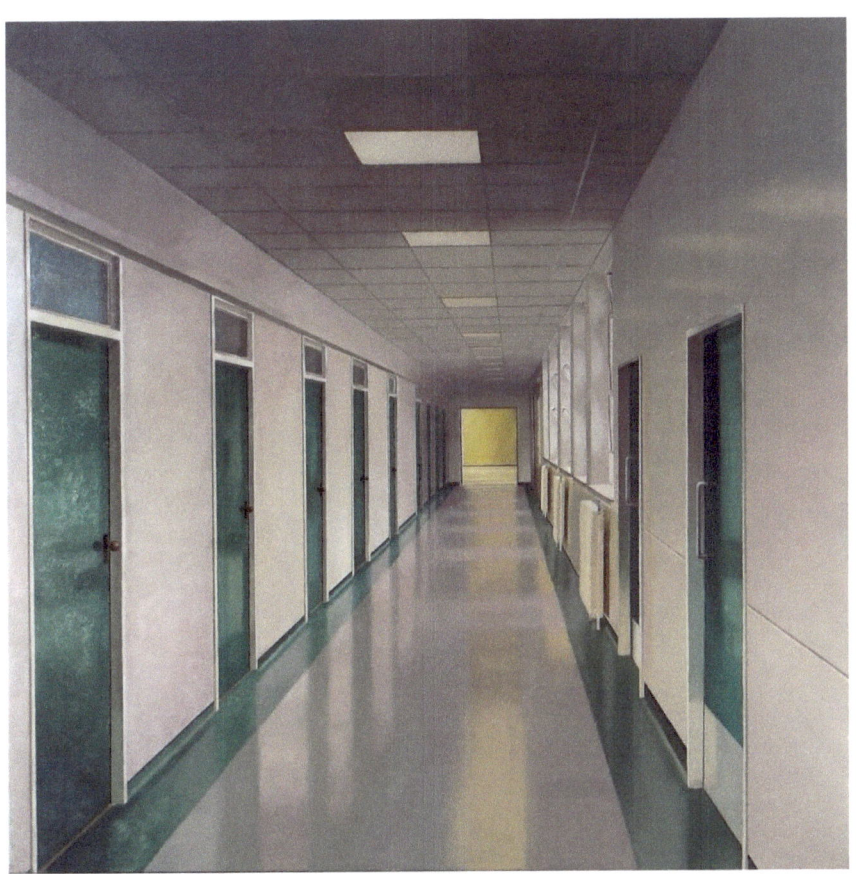

Critical Care 153cm x 153cm, Oil on linen, date 2004

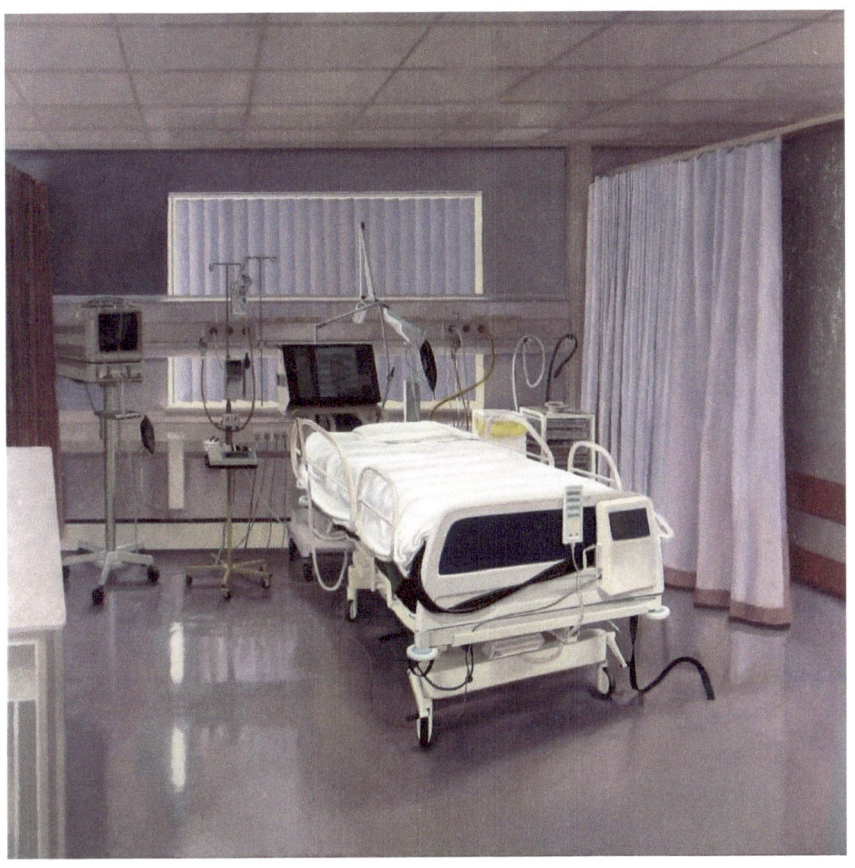

The Wellcome Collection, London

Operating Theatre 153cm x 153cm, Oil on linen, date 2004

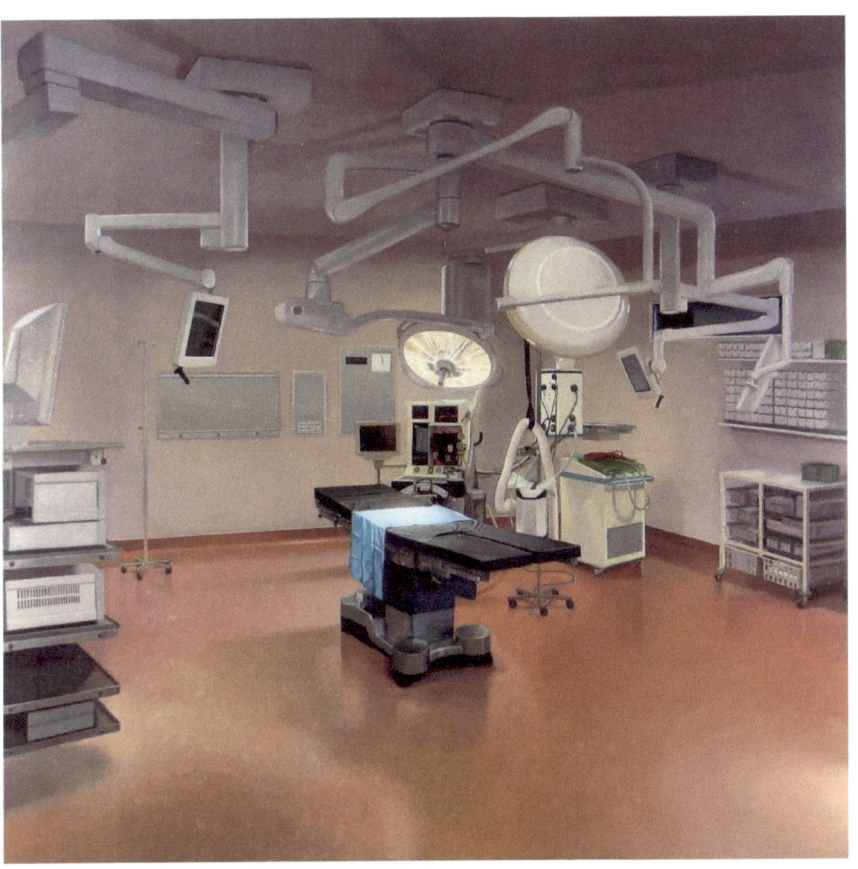

East Contemporary Art Collection, Ipswich

A Life Supported 183cm x 153cm, Oil on linen, date 2005

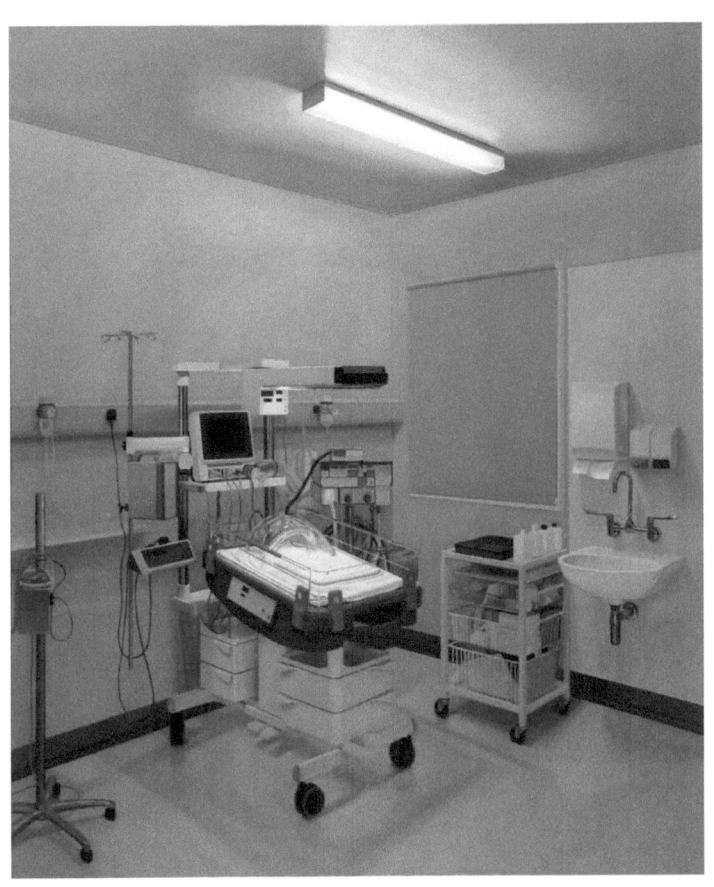

Threshold 153cm x 92.5cm, Oil on linen, date 2005

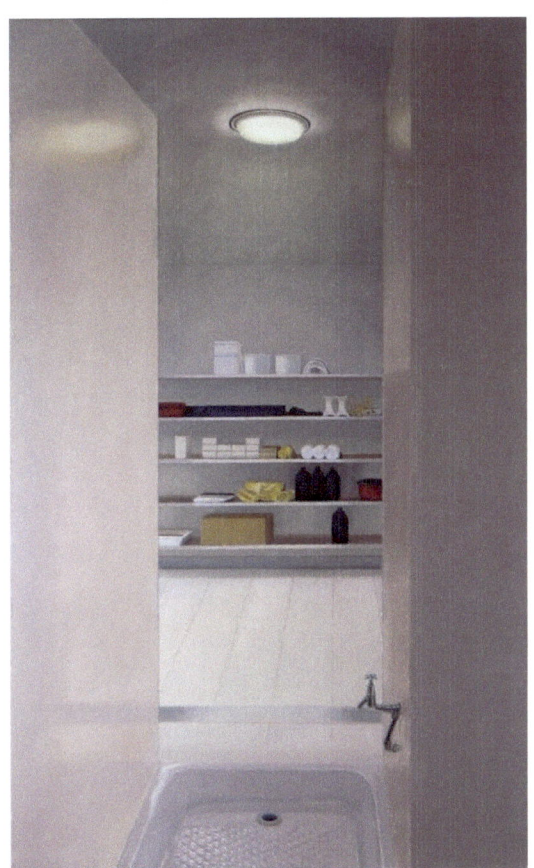

Mortuary 153cm x 183cm, Oil on linen, date 2005

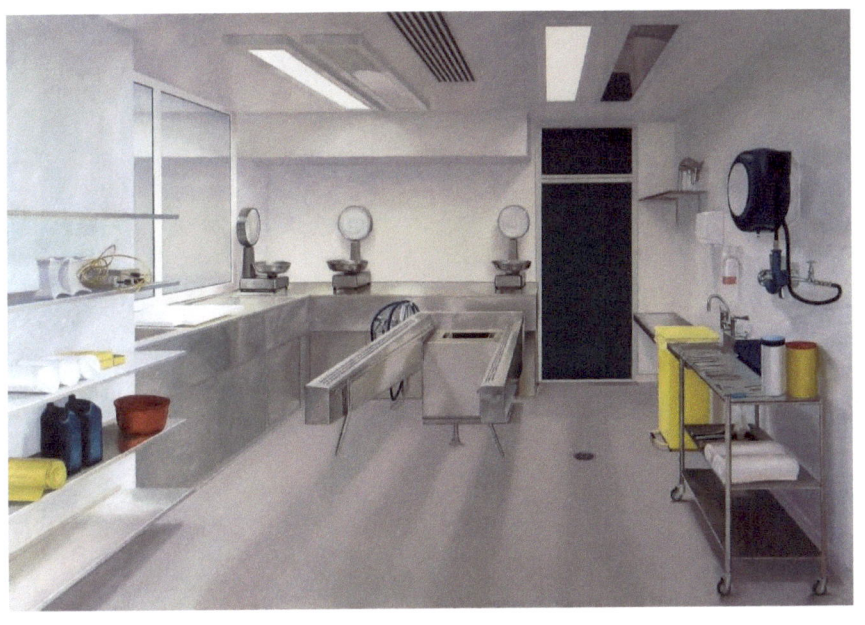

Body Storage 153cm x 153cm, Oil on linen, date 2004-5

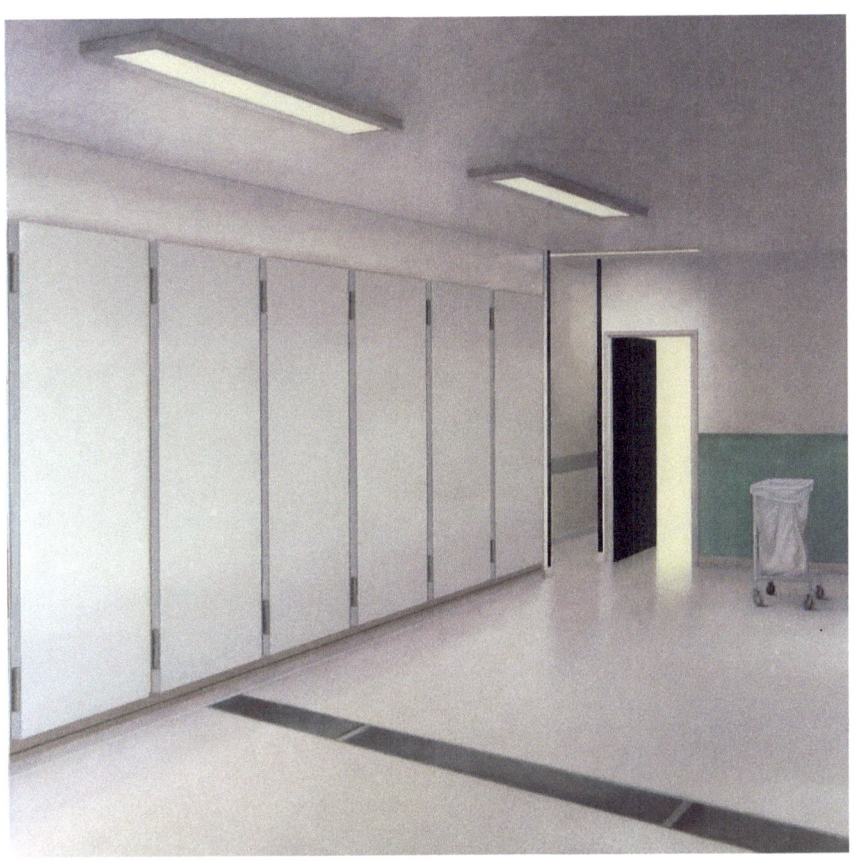

Collection of the Musée de Louvain-la-Neuve

Curving Corridor 153cm x 183cm, Oil on linen, date 2005

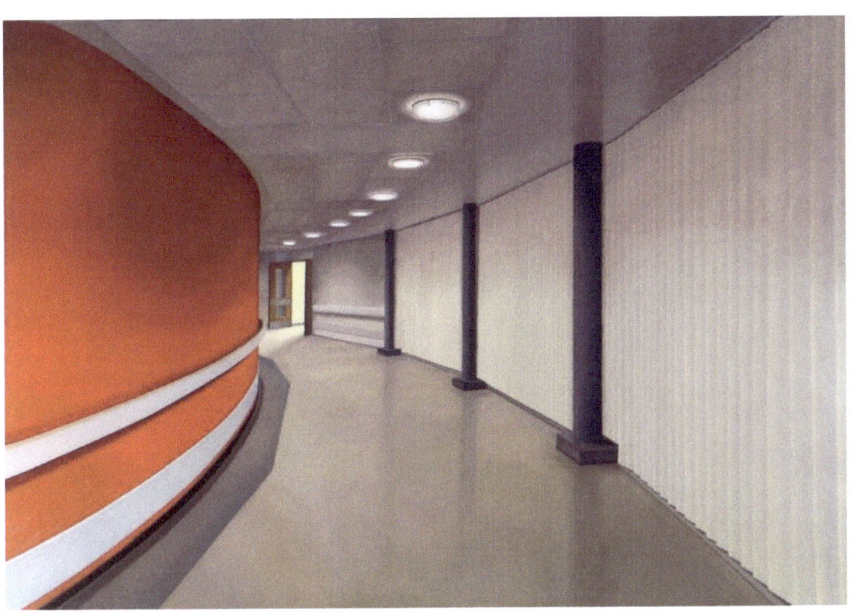

Afterword

The Hospital Series

In 2004 I set out to paint a series of pictures based on hospital spaces. Prior to this I had spent 12 years working as a portrait painter. During this time I began to concentrate on land and seascapes, and then, on artificially lit, man-made interiors. These formed the foundation for a series of paintings on Underground stations, which represented for me, places of emotional transition and disconnection.

In painting, I like to work on a large scale and make use of perspective to enable the viewer to gain a sense of being able to step into the room presented. I am interested in looking at the overlooked, and as this series developed, began to explore that which we may not wish to look at, at all. I became interested in rooms which are designed to perform their function with a matter of factness which overrides our emotional concerns.

In the eight hospital interiors I painted from 2004 – 2005, people are absent. The rooms are laid out ready for use. All signs, labels and regional references have been removed. The colours have been softened and harmonised. There are no views to the outside world and all the light is artificial. Life in these spaces is transitional.

Whilst superficially similar to the underground spaces, the hospital interiors introduced another dimension. Here, transitions are from one state to another and become loaded with a greater emotional significance. I am fascinated by the sense that some of our most extreme emotional experiences are encountered in the most sterile and emotionless of places.

In removing details from the scenes I represent, I aim to create a sense of a world like the real one, but one that is of the imagination. A parallel world that exists in our mind's eye. Whilst the real space can be threatening, the imagined one is seen at a safe distance, removed far enough away from real trauma, to enable contemplation.

When we use our minds eye to think we construct a mental picture built of the past. This picture for me is a projection of the past into the present. As we are drawn into an image, we can become aware of our feelings in relation to the world around us. We can use this process to imagine ourselves into the future. To think of ourselves beyond our current experience. For me, this links to the real experience of undergoing trauma and the minds ability to project into the future, to a time and place beyond the current.

In the 'Hospital' environments I imagine myself as the patient, stripped of my identity as father, husband, friend and citizen. I imagine myself reduced to a labelled body – a body to be cared for and processed in the hands of professionals. A body that exists at the mercy of others, a body over which I have no control.

The critical care bed for me, offers an extreme example of relinquishing control. It simultaneously offers a best and worst case scenario. The worst, because you would never wish to be in a state requiring that level of care, and the best, because in a life threatening situation you are at the best place you could possible be.

I am fascinated by the equipment used, the physical space occupied and the number of skilled people required to run it. I found the space around the bed given to enable a team to work on a patient in an emergency engaging. And, I am intrigued by the fact that everything is on wheels, emphasizing the temporary nature of a life in the balance, and in a broader sense, of all life. What especially interests me with the critical care environment is the expression given in a very physical sense to the service of maintaining life. It is a space in which all life is valued equally. That, no matter who you are, medical care for those at the receiving end provides an experience without hierarchy. We are all reduced to the status of child subject to the authority of our surgeon.

This leads me to a broader and more significant concept of the separation of the body from a sense of the self. The paintings in the 'Hospital' series focus on the practical aspects of dealing with the body. This acknowledges for me the body as a vessel which carries us, for which we are responsible, but over which we ultimately only have a limited control. We are unable to prevent its illness and decay. We are unable to prevent our bodies aging and dying.

They impose their demands upon us. The need to sleep, eat, drink, reproduce and empty our bowels. The body demands and we obey. What choice do we have? Some, we can choose when we sleep, eat and drink to an extent. In the critical care environment we are unable to exercise this small amount of control we enjoy. All pretence is gone. For me, illness reveals the body to be a prison which contains us. Our sense of self is separate from the physical self. Our bodies controlling major aspects of our life experience.

The sense of relinquishing control of the body offers an extension for me of relinquishing control over other aspects of life. I see the idea of exercising control over others as a route to personal unhappiness. Whereas, placing the needs of those around you before your own, leading to an ultimate contentment. In the 'Hospital' paintings I set out to extend my thinking on the removal of personal control and explore more fully the concept of absence as the memory of presence.

Robert Priseman, October 2007

Thanks Due:

Tony Bond
Dr Ben Cranfield
The Dittrick Collection
Jay Goldmark
Mike Goldmark
Dan Heider
Professor Margaret Iversen
Ally Seabrook
John Wallet
The Wellcome Trust